The G.R.E.A.T.E.S.T. Soul Journey

THE JOURNEY BEGINS WITH YOU.

KATHLEEN E. WALLS, PSY.D.

BALBOA.
PRESS

A DIVISION OF HAY HOUSE

Balboa Press books may be ordered through booksellers or by contacting:

Balboa Press
A Division of Hay House
1663 Liberty Drive
Bloomington, IN 47403
www.balboapress.com
1-(877) 407-4847

Because of the dynamic nature of the Internet, any web addresses or links contained in this book may have changed since publication and may no longer be valid. The views expressed in this work are solely those of the author and do not necessarily reflect the views of the publisher, and the publisher hereby disclaims any responsibility for them.

The author of this book does not dispense medical advice or prescribe the use of any technique as a form of treatment for physical, emotional, or medical problems without the advice of a physician, either directly or indirectly. The intent of the author is only to offer information of a general nature to help you in your quest for emotional and spiritual well-being. In the event you use any of the information in this book for yourself, which is your constitutional right, the author and the publisher assume no responsibility for your actions.

Any people depicted in stock imagery provided by Thinkstock are models, and such images are being used for illustrative purposes only. Certain stock imagery © Thinkstock.

Printed in the United States of America

ISBN: 978-1-4525-3234-9 (sc)
ISBN: 978-1-4525-3235-6 (e)

Balboa Press rev. date: 2/3/2011

This book has been dedicated to you.

I pray that you live your life to the highest Divine intention.
I pray that you know you deserve happiness and joy, and
that you can have them right now.
I pray that love and peace be within you and around you
at all times.
I pray that you know you are one with the Divine.
I pray this in the name of Divine Love.
Amen.

CONTENTS

INTRODUCTION

*H*umanity is the starting point on the way to Divinity. We are powerful and gloriously divine beings capable of more than we often allow ourselves to ever think or imagine. The G.R.E.A.T.E.S.T. Model created by Dr. Kathleen E. Walls assists people in restoring their understanding of who they are, encourages them to use their gifts and talents, and motivates them to live up to their Greatness. The G.R.E.A.T.E.S.T. stands for the following:

- •G: God
- •R: Restores
- •E: Excellence
- •A: Activates
- •T: Talents
- •E: Encourages
- •S: Spiritual
- •T: Transformation

This model will assist you in looking at your life, your relationship with yourself and others, your spiritual and religious thoughts and beliefs, and the ways in which you are working toward or against your goals. During the process, you will be led to release old thoughts, behaviors, and/or relationships that are no longer healthy or working toward your G.R.E.A.T.E.S.T. self. You will find yourself making sure your words, thoughts, and actions are matching. In order to fully engage in the process, it will be important to take some time to be still and reflect; therefore I encourage you to take what I refer to as a "PTO," Personal Time Out.

I often take PTOs. Sometimes these PTOs are by choice, such as when I find myself having a strong emotional reaction to something and/or when I keep getting "signs" or repetitive messages—you know, when you keep hearing the same thing over and over again. These are my signals to be still, listen, and examine the messages and lessons that are calling for my attention.

PTOs may also be in order when I start saying to myself, "I can't believe this is happening to me again," "Why me," "I thought I was doing better this time," etc. These familiar tunes usually signal that it is time for a change because I am either caught in a loop or headed in a direction that my G.R.E.A.T.E.S.T. self does not want to go.

Then, other times I am Divinely forced to take a PTO. This is when I have either unexpected or undesired time on my hands, such as sickness that seems to "come out of nowhere," a broken relationship, or a change in my job situation (one that I usually don't like), etc. Although this unexpected time and these undesired situations might not feel Divine, I believe that they are because they give me opportunities to grow, change, and better myself.

So let's begin this journey into self. As you walk through and plan your life, you may have to revisit thoughts, beliefs, and concepts because you will grow and change at each step of the way. What once was your life pattern may no longer fit into or align with your current-day personal truth.

Remember that this journey is about you and your moving forward in life. Take each step at your own pace. You will find that the G.R.E.A.T.E.S.T. process is ongoing and will evolve as you evolve. While you make the internal changes, the external changes will follow. So, if you're ready, let's start living your G.R.E.A.T.E.S.T. Life now.

CHAPTER 1

THE G.R.E.

*J*n the G.R.E.A.T.E.S.T. Model, the G.R.E. stands for God Restores Excellence. These first three steps were designed to help you "clear the clutter" in your life and remember your self-worth/personal value. Self-worth refers to how much you value yourself. Many times, people use the term self-esteem to refer to this concept. It is important for you to recognize your worth. You are priceless!

Throughout life, situations may have occurred that caused you to question your self-worth or personal value. These incidents may have also caused you to forget your true value and begin to live below your worth by choosing and accepting unhealthy and unproductive situations and/or relationships into your life. Therefore it is important to take a Personal Time Out, or PTO, and remember your self-worth/personal value.

Imagine if you were a $100.00 bill, and you were crumbled up, covered with mud, and put in the trash. Would your value change? No, you would still be worth $100.00, dirt and all; your value would still be retained. If you found this $100.00 bill, would you say, "It's no good and not worth anything because it's dirty"? Again, the answer is no, $100.00 is still $100.00.

It is true that some things in life have occurred to make you question or feel less than your value, but you must remember that a "little dirt" or negative experiences don't change your value. You are still and always will be priceless!

As you begin to reexamine your value and clean off the dirt (negative life experiences), you are being restored to excellence. Take a moment to reflect on the following concepts, and answer the questions to help you restore your understanding of your value.

GOD:

Creator, Lord, Christ, Allah, Buddha, Source, Universe

People from various parts of the world and cultures have different ideas and names for God. One's spiritual beliefs and foundation tend to guide one's personal and professional decisions, interactions, and relationships. These beliefs can also affect and influence our sense of self. Therefore it is important to have a clear understanding of the spiritual beliefs, concepts, and relationships that are driving many of your decisions and interactions. Think about your ideas or concepts of God and answer the following questions.

What have you been taught about "who God is and what God is really like"?

_____

_____

_____

_____

_____

_____

_____

_____

_____

_____

_____

_____

_____

_____

_____

_____

Think about and answer: "Who or what is God to you?" For example, do you think of/experience God as a judge, a father/mother, a punisher, or forgiving God? If you are unsure, that's okay. Remember, this not about being "right or wrong"; it is about you being clear on your relationship.

_____

_____

_____

_____

_____

_____

_____

_____

_____

_____

_____

_____

_____

_____

_____

How is what you have been taught about God similar to or different from how you experience God? In what ways?

_____

_____

_____

_____

_____

_____

_____

_____

_____

_____

_____

_____

_____

_____

_____

_____

_____

_____

Do you recognize God's presence in your life? If so, in what ways?

_____

_____

_____

_____

_____

_____

_____

_____

_____

_____

_____

_____

_____

_____

_____

_____

_____

Kathleen E. Walls, Psy.D.

Describe your current relationship with God.

_____

_____

_____

_____

_____

_____

_____

_____

_____

_____

_____

_____

_____

_____

_____

_____

_____

How does your concept and/or relationship with God influence your life (i.e., relationships, career, family, etc.)?

_____

_____

_____

_____

_____

_____

_____

_____

_____

_____

_____

_____

_____

_____

_____

_____

_____

What do you think/feel God wants for you in this life?

_____

_____

_____

_____

_____

_____

_____

_____

_____

_____

_____

_____

_____

_____

_____

_____

_____

What does the phrase "You are made in the image and likeness of God" mean to you?

_____

_____

_____

_____

_____

_____

_____

_____

_____

_____

_____

_____

_____

_____

_____

_____

_____

How do you think/feel God sees you?

_____

_____

_____

_____

_____

_____

_____

_____

_____

_____

_____

_____

_____

_____

_____

_____

_____

_____

The G.R.E.A.T.E.S.T. Soul Journey

How is the way that God sees you and feels about you similar to how you see and feel about yourself?

_____

_____

_____

_____

_____

_____

_____

_____

_____

_____

_____

_____

_____

_____

_____

_____

_____

How is the way that God sees you and feels about you different from how you see and feel about yourself?

_____

_____

_____

_____

_____

_____

_____

_____

_____

_____

_____

_____

_____

_____

_____

What do you need to do to be more like your positive "godly image"?

_____

_____

_____

_____

_____

_____

_____

_____

_____

_____

_____

_____

_____

_____

_____

RESTORES:

Back to original position/condition

When you think about the concept of "restoring" something, you think about returning it back to its original position or condition. Many times, people restore houses, buildings, cars, or furniture. The restoration is done in an attempt to "bring back" its original luster and shine, its original value. As you go through this process, you are remembering who you are, your value, your self-worth. You are being restored! Take the time to answer the following questions on your road to restoration.

The G.R.E.A.T.E.S.T. Soul Journey

Where in your life do you need to be restored/repaired?

_____

_____

_____

_____

_____

_____

_____

_____

_____

_____

_____

_____

_____

_____

_____

_____

_____

_____

_____

What steps do you need to take in order to make these repairs?

_____

_____

_____

_____

_____

_____

_____

_____

_____

_____

_____

_____

_____

_____

_____

How will you know when you have been restored? What will you look like? How will you feel? How will you behave?

_____

_____

_____

_____

_____

_____

_____

_____

_____

_____

_____

_____

_____

_____

_____

_____

_____

_____

_____

Kathleen E. Walls, Psy.D.

EXCELLENCE:

Excelling, being superior

In the Bible, it says that male and female were made in the image and likeness of God. However, we often "play down" our abilities. Some do this in an attempt to be humble or modest, while others don't truly recognize their abilities, competence, and value. Hence, we don't live up to or beyond our true potential, our Greatness. When we don't recognize or work toward our excellence, we are not living up to our G.R.E.A.T.E.S.T. self. So now is the time to shake off the humility and wear your coat of excellence.

In what areas of your life do you excel? What would you or others say you do extremely well (such as sing, teach, listen, organize, etc.)?

_____

_____

_____

_____

_____

_____

_____

_____

_____

_____

_____

_____

_____

_____

_____

_____

When and where are you currently using these "excellent" areas/skills in your life? If you are not using them, why have you chosen not to use these excellent skills?

_____

_____

_____

_____

_____

_____

_____

_____

_____

_____

_____

_____

_____

_____

The G.R.E.A.T.E.S.T. Soul Journey

When and where are you your G.R.E.A.T.E.S.T. self?

_____

_____

_____

_____

_____

_____

_____

_____

_____

_____

_____

_____

_____

_____

_____

_____

_____

_____

Identify the people in your life that you are with when you function as your G.R.E.A.T.E.S.T. self. Identify those who help and encourage you to be your G.R.E.A.T.E.S.T. self.

_____

_____

_____

_____

_____

_____

_____

_____

_____

_____

_____

_____

_____

_____

In what areas of your life would you like to improve? These may be areas that you already do well but want to do better (areas of strength). You may want to focus on areas that you would like to improve or strengthen (areas of "weakness"). Remember, weaknesses are areas that haven't been worked on—like a muscle that you haven't worked out, it's up to you to strengthen these areas. Identify the steps to take to improve these areas, and identify who can help you improve in these areas.

_____

_____

_____

_____

_____

_____

_____

_____

_____

_____

_____

_____

_____

_____

CHAPTER 2

MOVE & USE

The second phase of the G.R.E.A.T.E.S.T. Model is the Move & Use phase. The "A.T." stands for "Activates Talents." During this phase you are actively exploring, identifying, strengthening, and using your gifts and talents. At this time, you may find yourself wanting to participate in cooking, music, art, or dance classes. You may find yourself thinking about and being led to participate in hobbies that you either used to do as a child (i.e., fishing, sewing, etc.) or always wanted to do. Go for it!

This time may also spark an interest in changing careers or making a career out of your hobby. Hence, this may be a time of discovery, development, and/or remembrance. Overall, it is a time to put your gifts and talents to use.

ACTIVATES:

To set in motion/make more active

The word "activate" has a life and energy of its own. It denotes movement and action. Movement is important for our overall physical, spiritual, and emotional health and well-being. Like water that doesn't move, we too can become dormant and stagnant. Therefore it is important to keep the energy flowing and moving in the direction toward our G.R.E.A.T.E.S.T. self. Take this time to think of the areas in your life where you want and/or need to be more active.

In what areas of your life do you want or need to "set in motion"?

_____

_____

_____

_____

_____

_____

_____

_____

_____

_____

_____

_____

_____

_____

_____

_____

_____

What hobbies, interests, or skills keep coming to mind and want your active participation?

_____

_____

_____

_____

_____

_____

_____

_____

_____

_____

_____

_____

_____

_____

_____

_____

_____

What steps do you need to take to be more active in this/these area(s) of your life?

_____

_____

_____

_____

_____

_____

_____

_____

_____

_____

_____

_____

_____

_____

_____

_____

_____

Kathleen E. Walls, Psy.D.

What is preventing you from being more active in your life?

_____

_____

_____

_____

_____

_____

_____

_____

_____

_____

_____

_____

_____

_____

_____

_____

_____

_____

TALENTS:

Natural ability/ability of a superior quality

Here is another opportunity for you to recognize your Greatness. These are often referred to as your "God-given" gifts and talents because you have natural ability of superior quality. Each of us has been born with gifts and talents. I learned very early in life that I had an exceptional gift of listening. Once realized, I continued to develop this skill/talent and actively use it in my personal, professional, and spiritual life. Take some time to think about and identify your talents.

What are your natural talents? List the areas in your life that you do easily, without practice or training (for example, singing, event planning, listening, etc.)

_____

_____

_____

_____

_____

_____

_____

_____

_____

_____

_____

_____

_____

_____

_____

What would your family, friends, neighbors, and/or co-workers say are your talents? If you are not sure, ask them, and have them provide examples. Then, compare what they say to your own list. We are often more talented than we know or recognize.

_____

_____

_____

_____

_____

_____

_____

_____

_____

_____

_____

_____

_____

_____

_____

_____

What talents are you using?

_____

_____

_____

_____

_____

_____

_____

_____

_____

_____

_____

_____

_____

_____

_____

What talents are you not using? If you are not using them, why have you chosen not to use them? What is preventing you?

_____

_____

_____

_____

_____

_____

_____

_____

_____

_____

_____

_____

_____

_____

_____

_____

What talent(s) do you have that could benefit your family? Community? Society? The world? How?

_____

_____

_____

_____

_____

_____

_____

_____

_____

_____

_____

_____

_____

_____

_____

_____

What talents are you discovering? What are you doing to strengthen these talents?

_____

_____

_____

_____

_____

_____

_____

_____

_____

_____

_____

_____

_____

_____

_____

CHAPTER 3

BEYOND G.R.E.A.T.

*W*elcome to phase three! At this point, if you have completed the first two phases, you are G.R.E.A.T. and moving toward being the G.R.E.A.T.E.S.T. During this phase— in case you haven't noticed already—you may find that your life and thinking are changing. Have you also noticed changes in your spiritual awareness and practices?

At this time, many people begin to find themselves interested in exploring and learning about other spiritual practices or they have a deeper understanding and appreciation of their current spiritual practice. You may also find that you are interested in maintaining a balanced and honest life, tending to the needs of your mind, body, and spirit, as well as exploring how you can have a positive impact on others and the world.

It is important to remember that everyone responds to change differently. I often think of the process of change like growing pains that occur during puberty. For some, their knees or feet hurt, while others don't seem to experience any difficulties.

The same may occur here. Some of you (and those around you) may enjoy change and embrace it. For others, change may be uncomfortable and even frightening. At times during this process, you may find yourself moving out of what is "familiar" or comfortable, into unfamiliar territory. It is also important to note that during some parts of this journey, you may find yourself needing or wanting to spend some time alone, away from family and/or friends. Lastly, you may find your relationships with family and friends changing.

It is important to trust the process. Like a plant that is being pruned (cut back), at first it looks a mess, but afterward it is healthier, more plentiful, and even more beautiful.

ENCOURAGE:

To inspire with hope, courage, or confidence

When we think of the word "encourage," we are given messages of hope and confidence. We are led to "tap into" that place inside us that knows we are capable, that knows we are excellent and powerful. As we grow, we learn to encourage ourselves as well as others. At this point in the process, we are learning how to balance self-needs with the needs of others. Just as you are encouraged to live as your G.R.E.A.T.E.S.T. self, you are led to encourage others to do the same.

In what areas of your life have you received encouragement? By whom? How has it been helpful?

_____

_____

_____

_____

_____

_____

_____

_____

_____

_____

_____

_____

_____

_____

_____

_____

_____

In what areas of your life do you still need encouragement? Are you able to encourage yourself, or do you need encouragement from another source? If so, who? How is this encouragement going to be helpful to you?

_____

_____

_____

_____

_____

_____

_____

_____

_____

_____

_____

_____

_____

_____

_____

_____

Who is currently in your life (neighbor, family, friend, co-worker, etc.) whom you would like to encourage, or needs encouragement? In what ways would you like to encourage this person or these people?

_____

_____

_____

_____

_____

_____

_____

_____

_____

_____

_____

_____

_____

_____

SPIRITUAL:
Relating to God/affecting the soul

The concept of "spirituality" tends to refer to one's personal or direct relationship with the Highest Divine Source (God) and how this relationship affects our own soul/spirit. Just like the changing and growing nature of our familial relationships and friendships, our spiritual relationship grows and changes as well. Take some time to think about the ways in which you are nurturing and developing your spiritual relationship. The following questions focus on your soul/spirit development and expression.

In what ways have you been strengthening and/or increasing your relationship with God?

_____

_____

_____

_____

_____

_____

_____

_____

_____

_____

_____

_____

_____

_____

_____

_____

_____

In what ways are you strengthening your spiritual development (i.e., meditating, reading spiritual books, etc.)?

Are you living your soul's purpose? If so, how? If not, why aren't you? Are you waiting for something? If so, what?

_____

_____

_____

_____

_____

_____

_____

_____

_____

_____

_____

_____

_____

_____

_____

_____

Think about the ways that you desire to fulfill your soul's purpose. Do you want to help a certain group of people, start an organization, or write a book? In what ways have you been feeling led to make a difference in your life, your family, friendships, your community, the world?

_____

_____

_____

_____

_____

_____

_____

_____

_____

_____

_____

_____

_____

_____

List the ways that you would like to or are feeling led to express your soul (write poetry, sing, dance, paint, bake, be a volunteer in an organization, etc.).

_____

_____

_____

_____

_____

_____

_____

_____

_____

_____

_____

_____

_____

_____

_____

TRANSFORMATION:

A change in appearance or character for the better

At this point in the process, you may find that you are feeling different and even looking different. You may notice that you are not responding to situations the way you used to. What once used to make you angry, now doesn't faze you as much or, instead of keeping your feelings bottled up, you are able to express them in a loving way that frees you of the negative emotion and helps the other person grow in the process.

You realize that you want to be proud of yourself and your actions five minutes from now, five weeks from now, five months from now, and five years from now. When situations and interactions arise, you have a tendency to prefer to function out of your "highest divine self."

What personal transformation have you noticed about yourself? Are you responding to situations differently? Have you noticed that you look different? Are you taking steps toward a healthier lifestyle?

_____

_____

_____

_____

_____

_____

_____

_____

_____

_____

_____

_____

_____

_____

_____

_____

_____

You may be hearing repetitive messages about your calm or peaceful nature. Take this moment to think about and list the positive qualities that others have noticed or mentioned about you.

_____

_____

_____

_____

_____

_____

_____

_____

_____

_____

_____

_____

_____

_____

_____

_____

_____

What areas of your life would you like to transform?

_____

_____

_____

_____

_____

_____

_____

_____

_____

_____

_____

_____

_____

_____

_____

_____

_____

What steps do you need to take to assist yourself in this transformation?

_____

_____

_____

_____

_____

_____

_____

_____

_____

_____

_____

_____

_____

_____

_____

_____

_____

_____

_____

_____

_____

_____

_____

_____

_____

_____

_____

_____

_____

_____

_____

_____

_____

_____

_____

CHAPTER 4

LIVE YOUR LIFE
TO THE FULLEST

Now that you have worked on yourself and uncluttered your inner life, let's focus on your outer life. As you think about the words "life" and "living," it is important for you to think about your definition of life and what living means to you. This includes the various aspects of what you perceive to be a successful, prosperous, healthy, and productive life. Take some time to answer the following questions. Remember that "life" without the "f" (f = fullness) is a "lie." So live your full life.

Finish this thought: Life means ...

_____

_____

_____

_____

_____

_____

_____

_____

_____

_____

_____

_____

_____

_____

_____

_____

_____

The G.R.E.A.T.E.S.T. Soul Journey

You know that you are living your life when ...

_____

_____

_____

_____

_____

_____

_____

_____

_____

_____

_____

_____

_____

_____

_____

_____

_____

When you dream about your G.R.E.A.T.E.S.T. Life, what's going on? What do you see or envision? What does your life look like?

_____

_____

_____

_____

_____

_____

_____

_____

_____

_____

_____

_____

_____

_____

_____

_____

Who have you invited to be a part of your G.R.E.A.T.E.S.T. Life? Why have you chosen these people to be included in your G.R.E.A.T.E.S.T. Life?

_____

_____

_____

_____

_____

_____

_____

_____

_____

_____

_____

_____

_____

_____

Kathleen E. Walls, Psy.D.

What steps do you need to take to live a successful, prosperous, happy, healthy, and productive life?

_____

_____

_____

_____

_____

_____

_____

_____

_____

_____

_____

_____

_____

_____

_____

_____

CHAPTER 5

ASSESS YOUR LIFE

nce you have completed the previous exercises, you should see and feel a difference in yourself and in your life overall. Put a check mark next to each statement that is true and describe the differences that you are experiencing.

This is also a time to reflect on and identify the areas in your life that still need some attention and/or need to be changed.

_____ **Clarity:** *able to see clearly, easily understood*

_____ You are thinking more clearly.

_____ You are clearer on the steps needed to achieve your goal(s).

List additional areas of your life where you now have clarity.

_____

_____

_____

_____

_____

_____

Identify the areas in your life where you still need to achieve clarity, and identify the steps that will help to increase clarity in these areas.

_____

_____

_____

_____

_____

_____

_____ **Focused:** *aware and attentive*

_____ You are working toward your goals.

_____ You know what's motivating you.

In what other ways have you noticed that you have greater focus in your life?

_____

_____

_____

_____

_____

_____

_____

Where do you need to be more focused in your life?

_____

_____

_____

_____

_____

_____

_____

_____ **Expectant:** *eagerly awaiting, anticipating*
_____ You anticipate the best!
List the areas in your life where you are expecting the best.

_____

_____

_____

_____

_____

_____

_____

List the areas in your life where you need to expect the best (school, job, relationship, etc.). What needs to change so you can expect the best?

_____

_____

_____

_____

_____

_____

_____

_____

_____ **Self-Worth/Personal Value:** *how you value yourself*

     _____ You know you deserve the best.

     _____ You have a better appreciation of yourself.

     _____ You recognize an increase in your personal and/or professional value.

List the areas of your life and the ways in which your self-worth/value has increased.

_____

_____

_____

_____

_____

_____

Identify the areas where your self-worth still needs to be increased.

_____

_____

_____

_____

_____

_____

_____ **Honest:** *telling the truth, stating how you really feel*

        _____ You are able to have a more honest relationship with yourself.

        _____ You are able to have a more honest relationship with others.

Identify the ways in which you have been more honest with yourself and others.

_____

_____

_____

_____

_____

_____

Identify the areas and/or people in your life where you need to be more honest.

_____

_____

_____

_____

_____

_____

_____ **Courage:** *to act in accordance with your own beliefs/ to have the mental and/or spiritual strength to persevere and withstand difficulty or opposition*

> _____ You are able to ask for what you need and deserve.

> _____ You have the courage and energy to follow the positive direction of your soul/spirit.

> _____ You are able to release unhealthy behaviors, situations, relationships, and/or opportunities that are not a benefit to your life or moving you toward your G.R.E.A.T.E.S.T. self.

List the ways that you have been more courageous in your life.

_____

_____

_____

_____

_____

_____

_____

_____

_____

_____

Identify the areas in your life where you need to be more courageous and then list the steps that you need to take (i.e., changing jobs, confrontation, repairing relationships, etc.).

_____

_____

_____

_____

_____

_____

_____

_____

_____

_____

_____

_____

_____

_____

_____

_____

_____

_____ **Happy:** *experiencing pleasure and/or satisfaction, feeling that your desires are met*

_____ You experience satisfaction more often.

_____ You enjoy life more.

Identify the areas in your life where you are happy. Who are you with?

_____

_____

_____

_____

_____

_____

_____

Identify the areas in your life where you are waiting for your desires to be met (and expect that they will be met).

_____

_____

_____

_____

_____

_____

_____

_____ **Positive:** *free from doubt or negativity*

_____ You are able to focus more on the positive in situations.

_____ You are able to move past negative thoughts easier than before.

List the areas in your life where you have a more positive outlook.

_____

_____

_____

_____

_____

_____

_____

Identify the areas in your life where negative thinking is still occurring. What can be done to change this thinking?

_____

_____

_____

_____

_____

_____

_____ **Grateful:** *appreciative, thankful*

_____ You are able to express gratitude for the various aspects of your life, including people, situations, learning experiences, etc.

_____ You recognize that your success and accomplishments as well as your perceived failures and negative experiences all work together to lead you to your G.R.E.A.T.E.S.T. self.

List the areas in your life where you are grateful.

_____

_____

_____

_____

_____

_____

_____

_____

_____

_____

_____

_____

_____

_____ **Other:** Describe the other positive differences you notice in your life as well as where you still need to make some changes. Identify the steps that you need to take to improve in these areas.

_____

CHAPTER 6

TIME TO CELEBRATE

*N*ow that excellence has been restored and you are actively using your talents, as well as transforming your life and the lives of others in a positive and healthy way, it is time to celebrate. Remember this is about you. You are the G.R.E.A.T.E.S.T. and you deserve the G.R.E.A.T.E.S.T. celebration.

List all the ways that you are going to celebrate yourself. Come back and add to this list as much as you like.

_____

_____

_____

_____

_____

_____

CHAPTER 7

CONCLUSION

My hope is that this process has provided clarity for you. Through being still and reflecting, we are often able to shed light on our lives and situations, as well as make more useful and informed decisions about the purpose and direction of our life. As you continue growing toward your G.R.E.A.T.E.S.T. self, the aspirations which once were your ceiling will now become your floor and foundation on which you stand to aspire to greater heights.

I wish you love, light, and peace as you continue on this journey. God bless, and may you continue to live your G.R.E.A.T.E.S.T. Life.

ADDITIONAL THOUGHTS

*U*se the following pages as you would like. You may want to continue some thoughts here or even draw some pictures. Remember, this is your book and it is about you.

_____

_____

_____

_____

_____

_____

_____

_____

_____

ABOUT THE AUTHOR

 Dr. Kathleen E. Walls is the owner and founder of the G.R.E.A.T.E.S.T. Counseling & Consulting, located in Philadelphia, Pennsylvania. She is a psycho-dynamically trained and systems-oriented doctor of Clinical Psychology. Dr. Walls counsels, consults, coaches, and delivers interactive seminars and motivational speeches. She researches and develops strategic plans, programs, and curriculums for a wide range of civic, educational, healthcare, and business enterprises. Dr. Walls enjoys traveling domestically and internationally, embracing and facilitating cross-cultural exchanges, incorporating a holistic perspective in the development of leaders, mentoring young people, and helping people learn how to live their G.R.E.A.T.E.S.T. Life. Visit www.askdrwalls.com